MW00682255

Getting Your H

Gail and Dave Veerman

Tyndale House Publishers, Inc. • Wheaton, Illinois

This book produced with the assistance of The Livingstone Corporation

---

Library of Congress Cataloging-in-Publication Data

Veerman, Gail.
    Getting your husband to talk / Gail and David Veerman.
       p.   cm.
    ISBN 0-8423-1325-7
    1. Communication in marriage—United States—Miscellanea.
2. Marriage—United States—Miscellanea. 3. Marriage—Religious
aspects—Christianity—Miscellanea. I. Veerman, David II. Title.
HQ536.V39   1994
646.7'8—dc20   93-35793

Printed in the United States of America

99 98 97 96 95 94
9   8   7   6   5   4   3   2   1

Special thanks to . . .

> *Mitzie Barton*
> *Kathe Galvin*
> *Sally Loan*
> *Marty Long*
> *Eadie McMahon*

. . . for their creative ideas, sparkling personalities, and understanding husbands!

Introduction

HUSBANDS come in all shapes, sizes, and personality types . . . as do wives. And the unique marriage combination of each husband and wife yields a colorful assortment of challenges to marital harmony and unity. Yet many wives voice a common complaint that seems to rise above all others: "I can't get my husband to talk to me."

Some wives, of course, mean that literally—their husbands are virtually silent, keeping to themselves, brooding, holding thoughts and feelings inside.

For some wives, however, the problem involves busyness—hubby works from dawn to dusk and desires only to collapse and retreat to the newspaper or TV when he comes home.

And others mean that although their husbands seem to talk incessantly, like proverbial babbling brooks, the conversation usually borders on the superficial or boring. I mean, who really cares if Stinkleson hit four three-pointers in the play-off game? Or that some football team named after an animal had a good draft? Or that Washington streets are teeming with lazy bureaucrats? What about the kids, the house, the future?

If you see yourself in any of those descriptions, this book is for you. It won't ease all your interpersonal stresses and strains, but it will provide ways for you to get your husband talking.

See this as a smorgasbord of 101 ideas from which to choose. Try one that seems to fit your situation. Then try another. Get his attention, open the conversation, and get him talking.

Gail and Dave Veerman

1   Ask for advice.

Look for real (don't make these up) areas where your husband can give you help. Then ask him for it. For example, you might ask

- I have a problem with finding the time to take Sally shopping for school. What should I do?
- What suggestions can you give me for running the missions committee?
- What do you think I can do to balance my church and community involvement?

If he thinks you can learn from him, he will probably be willing to talk. He will also be more open to learning from you.

2 **Make the news.**

If your husband is in the habit of coming home from work and burying himself in the newspaper, write or type a personal message to him and tape it inside the newspaper where he can see it. Anything goes. The point is to get his attention.

Here are some starters
- Tell him you love him
- Tell him about something that happened today
- Ask for some information
- Ask for advice
- Tell a joke
- Ask him on a date
- Make an outrageous statement
- Ask a Trivial Pursuit question
- Ask if he knows what you're planning to do that evening

BONUS IDEA!

When he starts to talk, make eye contact with him.

3 Get really close.

If your husband is sitting in another room reading or watching television, sit very near him to watch the show or read your book. If possible, sit right next to him. Explain that you want to be close to him. Who knows? He may actually turn off the TV or put down the paper and turn toward you.

4 **Follow the steps.**

Before your husband comes home from work, cut out paper footprints and place them on the floor of the garage and house, leading from where he parks his car to where you want him to go. On the first step, write, "Step this way." At the end of the steps, have refreshments and comfortable chairs waiting for both of you. Sit with him and talk things over.

5   **Coach a team together.**

When the kids are into youth sports, often the husband is the
one who becomes the volunteer coach or assistant coach, and
the wife is just a spectator. Break the pattern by offering to
coach with your husband, even if you don't know much about
the sport. Your involvement will be especially helpful if it's a
team of girls. Besides spending time together before, during,
and after practices and games, you two can talk over game
strategy, player performance, your child's attitude, etc.

6   **Shock him.**

To get your husband's attention, say something that is an
exaggeration or that you know isn't true—something he will be
sure to react to. Choose a topic dear to his heart, such as his
favorite sports team, politics, or something related to work. See
how long you can make him believe you before you tell him
you're pulling his leg.

- I really think the Colorado Rockies have a good shot at winning the pennant, especially with their outstanding pitching staff!
- Did you know that Hillary Clinton is going to be the commencement speaker for Moody Bible Institute?
- According to the paper, mortgage interest rates should drop to 4 percent by the end of the year.
- We got a notice in the mail today that said our property taxes are going to double next year.

**BONUS
IDEA!**

Tell him a good joke.

Drive him there.

Look for uncustomary times when you and your husband can spend time together. A great possibility is in the car, driving your husband

- to his golf game
- to his bowling game
- home from the car dealer after dropping off the other car
- to his meeting at church
- on his errands around town

8   **Leave a message.**

Leave a message for your husband where he may least expect it. For example

- you could leave a note on the bathroom mirror
- if his car is dirty, you could write a message in the dust on the hood
- after a snow, you could write a message on the car or on the driveway

Your message could read, "I need to talk."

BONUS IDEA!

Expect him to talk more about events than emotions.

9 Serve fortune cookies.

After dinner, serve everyone fortune cookies and use the "fortunes" to spark conversation for the whole family. You could ask

- Why do some people believe these things?
- If you could know anything about the future, what would you like to know?
- If you could have a "real" fortune cookie (that is, the fortune would come true), what would you like the fortune to say?

To focus more on your husband, remove the fortune in the cookie and replace it with one of your own to get his attention. Make the fortune very specific. For example, you could type

- Your brown suit will serve you well when you meet with Cliff Johnson this Thursday
- Your wife, Marilyn, is a prize—don't lose her
- At 10 A.M. tomorrow, call [your phone number] for wonderful news.

10 Exercise.

Work with your husband on planning exercises and an exercise schedule that the two of you can do together. With walking, bicycling, cross-country skiing, and running, you can talk while you exercise. With swimming, tennis, and racquetball, you can talk as you go to and from the pool or court.

BONUS IDEA!

Never interrupt.

11 **Listen to a tape.**

Get tapes from well-known Christian speakers and authors, such as Steve Brown, R. C. Sproul, and James Dobson. After both of you have listened to a tape, talk it over.

12 **Change a room.**

One day when your husband is gone, completely change around a room in the house: the family room, bedroom, kitchen, etc. When he reacts to the change, explain that you wanted to shake things up a bit; then ask if there's anything in the house that *he* would like to change. Next, ask if there's anything in the family or in his life that he would like to change.

13 Ask, "What if . . . "

Think of imaginative questions about the future. Ask

- If we inherited $100,000, how do you think we should spend it?
- What would you do if you suddenly lost your job?
- What should we do if you were offered a great promotion but it meant moving far away from here?
- What would you do if the county exercised eminent domain and bought our house?
- If I suddenly died, what would you do to take care of the children?

- If you could hold any public office, what office would you choose? Why?
- If you could make three major changes in our church, what would you change? Why?

BONUS IDEA!

Feed him his favorite meal.

14 Ask questions about sports.

If your husband has a favorite sports team, do a little research
on the team and the sport and then ask him relevant questions.

- If he likes the Los Angeles Kings hockey team, you could ask
  about Wayne Gretsky and the Stanley Cup play-offs.
- If he follows the Chicago Cubs, you could ask about what
  they have to do to become pennant contenders.
- If he lives and dies with the Washington Redskins, you could
  ask what made Joe Gibbs such a great coach.
- If he loves golf, ask who he thinks are the top five
  professionals on the men's PGA tour and why.

15 **Discuss a book.**

Suggest a book to read that would interest both of you. Read it separately, and discuss a chapter at a time. Or read it to each other after dinner. Or get a taped version of the book and listen to it while you commute or do housework or jog.

Some popular Christian books
- *Beside Every Great Dad* by Nancy Swihart and Ken Canfield
- *Laugh Again* by Chuck Swindoll
- *This Present Darkness* by Frank Peretti
- *No Wonder They Call Him the Savior* by Max Lucado
- *When God Doesn't Make Sense* by James Dobson.

Other books you might enjoy

- *The Seven Habits of Highly Effective People* by Stephen Covey
- *What Color Is Your Parachute?* by Richard Nelson Bolles
- Mysteries by P. D. James or Dorothy L. Sayers
- Adventures by John Grisham or Tom Clancy
- Historical fiction by Bodie Thoene or Gilbert Morris
- The Chronicles of Narnia by C. S. Lewis
- The Lord of the Rings trilogy by J. R. R. Tolkein.

16 **Change the meal.**

- Surprise your husband by serving a special meal that features all of his favorite foods, even if they don't normally go together.
- Another time, serve dinner buffet-style, featuring leftovers from the last week with two or three special treats thrown in.
- Or have a theme meal, coordinating decorations, music, food, and dress. Themes could include love, Italy, spring, memories, Halloween, sports, or Bible characters.

BONUS IDEA!

Don't let the kids interrupt.

17 Focus on a shared value or goal.

Begin a conversation by relating what you want to say to a value or goal that your husband feels strongly about. For example, you could say

- Because I know you want our kids to have a good education, I thought we ought to talk about . . .
- I realize how concerned you are about our financial security; therefore, I thought we should discuss . . .

Of course what follows needs to relate—don't say something like: "Because I know you love the kids so much, I knew you'd be interested in talking about redecorating the kitchen." People will talk about anything that relates to what they hold dear. That even goes for your husband.

18 **Time yourselves.**

If you sense that your husband is afraid that the conversation will take too much time or that he won't be able to break through your sentences with a word or two of his own, offer to limit the time that each of you can talk. Set a timer for the agreed amount of time and begin talking. When the buzzer sounds, stop talking, reset the timer, and let him begin. Continue until your total time is up.

19 **Find a magazine article.**

As you read magazines such as *Christian Parenting Today*, *Focus on the Family* magazine, *Moody* magazine, and *Today's Christian Woman*, look for articles that might spark your husband's interest and a conversation. For example, you might find a lighthearted look at family vacations, an insightful piece on raising early adolescents, or a challenging column on family finances.

BONUS IDEA!

Turn off the car radio.

20 **Design love coupons.**

Many couples collect discount coupons for restaurants, grocery stores, and other retail businesses. Put together your own collection of discount coupons, and give them to your husband. Each coupon should be on a separate piece of paper or index card.

Here are some possibilities
- Good for one back massage—FREE
- Good for one dessert of your choice—FREE
- Good for 50 percent off any griping I might do when you're watching sports on TV
- Good for being 90 percent right in an argument
- Good for one hour of my help doing one of your jobs around the house
- Good for one extra helping of the entree at dinner

21 **Understand his world.**

Work hard at trying to understand your husband's interests, especially his job. Learn more about what his work entails, and remember names. Ask what he is doing and how it is going. Then listen. Once the conversation is started, who knows in what direction it may turn?

22 **Find a good cartoon.**

Many Christian magazines such as *Leadership Journal* and *Campus Life* feature hilarious cartoons about family and church life. Check those magazines, or look for books of cartoons in your local Christian bookstore. Cut out or photocopy a cartoon that you know your husband would appreciate and hand it to him, slip it in the newspaper, place it under his dinner plate, or stash it in his briefcase. Later, ask what he thought, and discuss how true to life the cartoon is.

BONUS IDEA!

Don't try to get him to talk when he's
exhausted. Give him time to rest first.

23 **Wait.**

Sometimes the best way to get your husband to talk is to be patient and wait for the right opportunity. When he gives signals that he wants to discuss something or open up about an area in his life, drop what you're doing, don't interrupt, and *listen.*

24 **Change roles.**

Choose the best time for both of you, and switch roles for a weekend. In other words, if usually he cuts the lawn and you clean the house, have him do the cleaning while you do the cutting. If a typical weekend for you involves chauffeuring the kids to their lessons and activities while he balances the checkbook and pays the bills, let him do the driving while you do the financial juggling. Besides giving you an appreciation for the other person's work, it will give you something to talk about on Sunday.

25   **Celebrate a holiday.**

With your husband, choose an obscure holiday to celebrate as a family. This could be anything from Groundhog Day or Columbus Day to a declaration by the mayor, governor, or president (for example, Chocolate Day, National Secretaries' Week, Corn Day, and National Pizza Day). Together plan the activities for the day and what you can talk about as a family at the end of your celebration.

26 **Offer to answer any question.**

Make a "question envelope" into which both you and your husband can put any question you want the other one to answer. Choose a regular time of the day or week when you will each draw out a question and answer it honestly. Or predetermine a time when you will both answer all the questions in the envelope.

BONUS IDEA!

Greet him with a smile and silence–
let him say the first word.

27 **Tour the house.**

Take your husband on a tour of the house. Stop in each room and pray for the lives most touched by that room, the activities that happen there, and anything else related to that room. For example, in the dining room you could thank God for all his provisions and pray for the entertaining that you will do there, that your guests will enjoy themselves and see Christ through your loving hospitality. And in your finished basement, you could pray for your children and their friends who will spend time there. This should lead to conversation about family and how you can use your home to glorify God.

28   **Play hearts.**

Place a deck of cards between you, face down. Take turns drawing cards and placing them face up next to the deck. Every time a person draws a heart, he or she must tell something personal about himself or herself that the other person doesn't know.

29 **Make a list.**

During the day, write down everything that you need to talk about with your husband. Then, at the appropriate time, say something like, "I have seven things I need to talk to you about." By saying that, you let your husband know that you are prepared. This will motivate him to help you polish off your list.

BONUS IDEA!

Never cut short a conversation to take a phone call.

30 Take a trip down memory lane.

Ask, "Remember when . . . "

- we walked barefoot in the park?
- I told you I was pregnant?
- we ate at that little seafood restaurant on the coast?
- we made snow angels?
- we dressed up for Mardi Gras?
- you told me we were being transferred?
- my father died?
- the doctor said your mom made it through the operation?
- you were showing off for me and broke your arm?
- you accepted Christ as your Savior?
- we took tennis lessons together?

31 **Pig out.**

After the kids are in bed, pull out the chips, popcorn, cake, or ice cream and pig out together. As you wolf down the snacks, you'll find much to talk about. (Hint: If you do this often, substitute carrot sticks and celery!)

32 Give compliments.

One caricature of wives is that they "nag, nag, nag"; in other words, the only time husbands hear from them is when something is wrong or when they need something done. Break this mold by looking for ways to affirm your husband. Try to catch him doing something right, and then tell him how much you appreciate it. This will help set a positive tone in your relationship and pry open the communication door.

Here are some things you can affirm your husband for. The more specific you can be, the better.

- something he did for one of the children
- something he did to lead the family spiritually
- a task he stuck with until it was finished
- long hours spent on a household project
- clothes that look good on him
- several pounds lost
- an act of kindness to a child or an animal
- letting his feelings show

BONUS IDEA!

Get him a drink and watch
him drink it.

33 **Have a virtual date.**

Before your husband goes on a business trip, agree ahead of time on a movie that you will both see at the same time while he's away. Afterward, call him up at his motel and talk about the movie.

34 **Make a card.**

To get your husband's attention or to communicate your desire
to talk, make a creative card. You can
- cut letters out of magazines
- make a collage
- write on old wallpaper
- mount an old photo
- clip a cartoon

35 Divide and conquer.

When you go to a fast-food restaurant, put the kids at one table (if they're old enough to take care of themselves), while you and your husband sit at another table. You won't have a *long* time to talk, but you will have some uninterrupted time.

BONUS IDEA!

Laugh with him, not at him.

36   **Read each other's mind.**

This game begins with one person saying, "I'm thinking of a time when . . . " and then adding a general phrase at the end. For example, you could say, "I'm thinking of a time when you were very excited" or "I'm thinking of a time when I was embarrassed." Then your husband asks a series of yes or no questions to try to determine what event you are thinking of. When he thinks he knows, he makes a guess. Award one point for every question asked and five points for every incorrect guess. Take turns making the statements and guessing. Eventually, the person with the lowest total points wins.

37 **Make predictions.**

Give your husband a sheet of paper, and have him make specific predictions about the future. You also make predictions about the same things. Put your predictions in an envelope marked with today's date. Review them whenever you want a good laugh.

The predictions could include
- Where will we be living in five years?
- Who will be the next president of the United States?
- Who will win the NBA championship?
- When will our daughter have her first date?
- What will our son say to us as soon as he comes home tonight?
- How many (grand)children will we have ten years from now?
- What will our family income be in ten years?

38 **Be positive.**

If you want to talk about something negative, begin the
conversation with at least one positive comment.

BONUS IDEA!

Don't argue your point until you're sure he's done stating his.

39 **Set an appointment.**

Get your husband's date book and schedule an appointment with him for yourself. At the appointed time, take him by the hand and lead him to a quiet place where you won't be interrupted—the deck, the porch, his home office, your bedroom. Then catch up on whatever you haven't had time to talk about.

Some topics to talk about
- how his work has been going
- how your work has been going
- what the kids have been doing
- where you want to go on your vacation
- money—making it, keeping it, spending it
- problems
- dreams
- bright ideas

40 **Make beautiful meals together.**

Get in the habit of preparing the evening meal together or, at least, cleaning up afterward together. It's amazing what comes up in conversation over a hot stove, grill, or sink.

BONUS IDEA!

Walk the dog together.

41 Use multiple choice.

If you have a topic that you need to talk about with your husband, ask him an intriguing question, and give him a number of answers from which to choose. For example, you could ask, "Where would you like to go on vacation this summer?" Possible answers could include (a) to the lake again, (b) camping out west, (c) to my parents' home, (d) around the world in 80 days, (e) all of the above, (f) none of the above, (g) one you haven't mentioned yet.

42 **Prepare an agenda.**

Agree on a time to talk things over. Beforehand, type up an official-looking agenda, complete with minutes from the last meeting and a treasurer's report. Before jumping into the items on the agenda, see if there is any other old or new business. Then work your way through the agenda, one item at a time. (This reassures some husbands who fear that the conversation may otherwise never end.)

43 **Hide notes.**

Write clever little notes and hide them where your husband will find them: in his lunch, under his pillow, in his briefcase, etc. If he doesn't bring it up, ask if he found your notes and what he thought of them.

The notes could be
- expressions of love
- jokes
- cartoons
- riddles
- reminders
- memories
- quotations
- Bible verses
- questions

BONUS IDEA!

Send the kids to camp.

44 **Work together.**

Offer to help your husband with his weekend tasks if he will help you with yours. Then you can do laundry, wash the car, bake a cake, cut the lawn, vacuum and dust the house, and repair the fence together. Doing things together is a giant step toward communication.

45 **Scare him.**

This is a variation of "Shock him." Say something about yourself or the kids, such as

- I'm thinking of going back to school to get my M.B.A.
- I think home schooling would work for us—we could share the teaching responsibilities.
- Junior has painted his bedroom flat black.
- The doctor says it's triplets.

Some husbands are frightened into conversation if they think their wives are losing it. You might try

- I think I saw Elvis at the supermarket yesterday.
- I just balanced my checkbook, and the bank thinks I have a thousand dollars in my account that I know nothing about.
- Now that the backyard is fenced, I believe I'll buy a horse.
- We're having turnips for dinner.

BONUS IDEA!

Drive to dinner in a town three hours away.

46 **Play his favorite songs.**

Buy a CD or cassette of hits from your husband's high-school years. Surprise him by playing it in the background during a meal. Then reminisce about high school. Talk about the misconceptions kids have about life, how people change over the years, and what happened to your classmates.

47 **Give him a call.**

On the weekend or in the evening, when your husband is at home watching TV or puttering and muttering and not paying much attention to you, go next door, to a cellular phone, or to a pay phone and give him a call. Pretend that you're taking a survey and ask for his opinion on various issues. If he recognizes your voice right away, explain that you just wanted to talk. Make an appointment for a conversation.

48 **Hear the sounds of silence.**

Explain to the family that for two hours the house must be totally silent (no radios, no televisions, no tape or CD players, no talking). Family members may communicate, but only through hand motions or writing. Afterward, talk about the experience as a family. After the kids have gone to bed, talk about it further with your husband (what he thought about, how noisy life gets, the effects of all the noise on the kids, etc.).

BONUS IDEA!

Wash the car together.

49 **Have a Bible study.**

Buy a couple of copies of a Bible study on a book of the Bible that you both would like to study together. Christian bookstores have many excellent resources, including the Life Application Bible Studies (Tyndale House Publishers). Cover one lesson a week. Take turns leading and teaching the lesson.

50 **Go *Back to the Future*.**

Some day when you and your husband are home alone
together, suggest to him that you go "back to the future."
Describe a scenario that could happen to you. Talk about what
you would do or what you wish you had done. You can do this
as a conversation or on paper. Sometimes it's helpful to jot
down ideas on paper and then talk about them.

Some scenarios for "back to the future"

- You know you will die within six months. What do you wish you had talked about with your spouse? What do you wish you had done differently? What memories make you glad?

- You are ready to retire. What do you remember as the high points of your working life? What do you wish you had done differently?

- You are very old and wise, and your children have come to you for advice. How will you tell them to conduct their lives? What would you tell them about marriage? About family? About faith?

51 Take a commercial break.

When your husband is watching a sporting event on TV that will last a while, see if he will agree to talk with you during the commercials. When the commercials come on, turn off the sound and talk. When the game comes back on, stop the discussion and turn up the sound. Continue your conversation at the next commercial break.

**BONUS
IDEA!**

End every day by praying together.

52 **Present a moral dilemma.**

Ask your husband a moral or ethical question. Listen to what he says he would do. Tell him what you think you would do. Are there differences? Why would you react differently?

Sample moral dilemmas

What would you do if . . .

- you found a roll of hundred-dollar bills in the park and no one was around?
- you learned that your boss was involved in illegal activity?
- an important business client wanted you to take him to a pornographic movie?
- you discovered that your child was involved in illegal activity?
- a cashier gave you five dollars too much in change? How about one dollar? How about ten cents?
- a friend told you something in confidence and later you discovered that your boss would really like that information?

53 **Lie on the floor.**

Lie on the floor in the family room, or on a warm night, lie on the ground and look at the stars. Use that time to unwind and talk about the day, your future plans, and anything else that comes to mind.

54 **Play a child's game.**

Pull out one of the games that your children used to play (for example, Chutes and Ladders, Sorry!, or Head of the Class). Talk about your kids, what you've learned over the years about parenting, and what you can do to have fun as a family these days.

BONUS IDEA!

Invite friends over for an old-fashioned sing-along.

55 **Go for a ride.**

Explain to your husband that you want to take him for a ride. Then drive to a nearby park or to the edge of a large parking lot, park the car, turn toward your husband, and explain that you want to talk with him for a few minutes. To avoid having him feel threatened, quickly explain that you just wanted to get away from the house and its distractions and communication barriers so that you could have a good conversation.

56 **Put up a sign.**

On a large piece of poster board, write in large letters, SEX. Place the sign somewhere in the house where your husband is bound to see it (in the garage, in the kitchen, in front of the TV, in the bedroom, in his closet). Note: If you have small children, put the sign where he will see it but they won't! When he asks what the sign is all about, explain that you were just trying to get his attention. Then bring up the subject you really wanted to talk about.

57 **Go to a marriage weekend.**

A number of Christian organizations offer retreats for couples or special seminars on marriage (for example, Marriage Encounter or Marriage Enrichment). Go together as a couple—it's almost guaranteed to get you talking.

BONUS IDEA!

Go on a picnic together.

58 Make a deal.

If you're having trouble tearing your husband away from the television, paper, or another interest, explain that you'll make him a deal. You'll stop bugging him and let him watch the game uninterrupted (or read for a half an hour uninterrupted), if he'll spend the hour afterward (or half an hour) talking with you.

59 Tell jokes.

Buy a book of puns and other corny jokes. Tell your husband the first half of the joke, and see if he can figure out the punch line. Or, if he's really good, tell him the punch line and have him figure out the question.

Some terrible puns

- In the Bible, where did they first sleep five in a bed? (Abraham slept with his forefathers)
- What's a Cajun lawn tool? (Black and Decker ["blackened decker"])
- What does Santa do in his garden? ("Hoe, hoe, hoe")
- What did the man ask when he learned that his neighbor would be vacationing in Hawaii? (Are you goin' t' Maui? [tomorrow])
- What do you get when you put 250 female pigs in a pen with 250 male deer? (500 sows and bucks [500,000 bucks])

60 Tell him about the call.

To get your husband's attention, casually mention that the IRS called. After he reacts, explain that IRS stands for

- I'm Really Searching
- I Require Sympathy
- I Reveal Secrets
- I've Repudiated Solitude
- I'm Repenting Slowly
- some other phrase you create

Explain that you and he need to talk . . . and it won't tax his brain.

Invite friends over for charades.

61   **Come back from the "store."**

Get a number of empty boxes and put them in shopping bags.
As your husband is relaxing, bring the bags in and explain that
you couldn't resist all the sales, but he should be happy with
all the money you saved. When he begins his lecture about
shopping and spending money, interrupt him and show him
that the boxes are empty. Then talk together about your
family's spending priorities.

62 Be a sweetheart.

Prepare his favorite dessert. After the kids have gone to bed,
invite him into the kitchen for a special surprise. Seat him at
the table with his eyes closed. Then put the dessert in front of
him and tell him that he can look. As you have dessert
together, talk over the sweet things you can do for each other
and for the kids.

63 **Pursue trivia.**

Get out your Trivial Pursuit game and just use the cards to quiz each other. Keep points if you wish to determine a winner. But as you play, look for conversation starters.

BONUS IDEA!

Go to an auto show together.

64 **Check the tabloids.**

On a visit to the supermarket, write down the headlines of various tabloids sold at the checkout counter. Mix in a few of your own. Read the headlines to your husband and see if he can tell the real ones from the fake ones. You'll probably start talking about how tabloids can get away with printing such crazy stuff and why people buy them.

Possible made-up headlines (assuming they are not at your supermarket this week)

- Two-Headed Alien Claims to Be Elvis's Son
- Baby Born with No Skin
- Secret Animal Cult Discovered in Rockies—Followers Worship Skunks
- Noah's Ark Discovered in Hollywood Hills
- Peanut-Butter Eating Dinosaur Makes Appearance in Georgia Classroom
- Moses' Body Comes to Life and Hurls Stones at Lebanese Militia

65 **Go on a fabulous date.**

Plan something really special for just the two of you to do: dinner at a fine restaurant, a concert you will both enjoy, a drive to the beach or to the mountains, or even a weekend package at a hotel. Make all the arrangements and reserve a spot in your husband's schedule. Then take him on the date.

Later, over dinner, dessert, or coffee, talk about
• what attracted you to each other when you first met
• when you realized you were in love
• what you've learned about each other over the years
• what counsel you would give to couples thinking of marriage

**Tell him you're the fairy godmother,
and ask what his three wishes are.**

66 **Read the paper.**

Scan the editorial page and find a columnist with an insightful, profound, or provocative editorial. Cut it out and give it to your husband to read. Then talk together about what the columnist wrote.

67 **Be playful.**

Parents often are playful with their kids, but not with each other. Have fun with your husband. Sneak up on him and give him a kiss . . . or tickle his ribs . . . or throw a water balloon at him on a hot day when he's cutting the lawn . . . or suggest that you see who can catch the most M&M's in his or her mouth. Laughing can break the ice for meaningful conversation.

68 **Write your feelings.**

Give your husband three sheets of paper and a pen. Take three
sheets and a pen for yourself too. Explain that on one sheet
you each should answer the question: How do I feel about
myself? After writing for about ten minutes, exchange papers
and discuss what you wrote. Next, on the second sheet of
paper, each of you should answer the question: How do I feel
about my spouse? Again, after about ten minutes, exchange
papers and talk about what you wrote. Finally, you each should
answer the question: How do I feel about God? Exchange
papers, read, and talk.

BONUS IDEA!

Go to the county fair together.

69 **Check out the yearbooks.**

Dig out the high-school yearbooks, sit on the couch next to each other, and leaf through the books together. Talk about what you were like back then and how you've changed. Talk about your spiritual life back then and how your relationship with God has matured.

Use study questions.

Choose a book on marriage that has study questions at the end of each chapter. Work out a schedule where you both read the same chapter and then answer the study questions together. Check out *Husbands and Wives* (Victor Books) for a number of excellent quizzes, inventories, and discussion questions.

71 **Pray together.**

In the car, on Sunday afternoon, before falling asleep, or during a lull in the frenetic activities, suggest that you two spend a couple of minutes praying together. Begin by writing a short prayer list. You could say, "What can I pray for you about?" Keep the list personal. Then pray. Afterward you can ask, "What else can we do about . . . " Also, promise to pray for his concerns during the day, when he is on a business trip, etc.

BONUS IDEA!

Play tiddlywinks.

72 **Listen to kids' music.**

This is especially appropriate if you have teenagers. During the day, tape a number of songs on the popular top-forty station. Go to a record store and get a listing of the top ten to fifteen rock and rap songs. Play the songs for your husband and show him the list. Talk about

- how music has changed since you both were teenagers
- what makes the records so popular
- what kids learn from listening to the songs
- how you can help your kids fill their minds with what is good and positive, instead of garbage

73 **Make lists.**

Suggest that you each make two lists: "What I like about you" and "What I don't like about you." (Note: This is especially appropriate during a disagreement or argument.) Take turns reading the "don't like" lists to each other. Then read the "like" lists. Talk through the items on your lists. Also discuss which list was easier to write and why.

74 Go on a mystery date.

Plan a special evening when you and your husband can go on a date. Make sure he leaves room in his schedule for your surprise. When the time comes, tell him what to wear. Then blindfold him, lead him to the car, and drive to the location (restaurant, bowling alley, theater, miniature golf course, etc.). If he doesn't have to worry about where you'll be going or what you'll be doing, he'll be more relaxed than usual and more open to conversation.

BONUS IDEA!

If he says something, stop what
you're doing and listen.

75 **Remember when.**

Play this memory game with your husband. Choose a category,
such as

- college
- when we were dating
- our family vacations
- our first house
- when the kids were babies

Then take turns reminiscing, beginning each memory with
the phrase, "I remember when . . ." or "I remember when you
. . ." (Note: You might want to begin by writing out your
memories, listing everything you can think of in five minutes,
and then reading your lists to each other.)

76 **Make a tape.**

If your husband drives to work and has a cassette player in his car, tape a message for him that he can listen to on his way to work. Take the positive approach on your tape—tell him you love him, tell him a joke, sing him a song, or do whatever will cheer him up for the commute. Ask him the questions that you need answered, or tell him the things that have been on your mind that you want to share with him. Encourage him to dictate a tape to you or to talk over your concerns with you when he returns.

77 Go golfing.

If your husband enjoys golf, suggest that you go with him for a round. If you don't play, just accompany him, helping him see where he hits the ball and then helping him find it. If he rents an electric cart, offer to drive the cart for him.

Read a devotional book together
every morning.

78 **Set aside the time.**

Explain that the two of you need to take some time to plan and to talk things over. Then set aside half a day. If you need to, go to a quiet place such as your church, a park, a friend's basement, a coffee shop, an office conference room, etc.

79 Buy a present.

You know better than anyone else what your husband needs and wants. And you know the difference between the two. Go shopping and buy him something he wants. It doesn't have to be expensive. Good gifts could include

- a golf glove
- a paperback book
- a pen
- a T-shirt from his favorite sports team
- a CD

Wrap it and then give it to him at dinner with the explanation that it's for being such a great husband. That ought to open him up.

80 **Make plans.**

Tell your husband that you want to imagine with him. Ask him to think of the dream home he would have if money were no object. Where would it be? What would it look like? How would it be furnished? As he speaks, mentally compare his ideas and dreams with yours. Don't tell him your dreams until he has finished telling you his.

BONUS IDEA!

Eat messy food together.

81 **Write your questions.**

Write down a question and give it to your husband. Ask him to answer in writing or orally, whichever he prefers. Be sure not to ask questions that can be answered with just one word, such as yes or no. You want him to talk in paragraphs, not grunts. Encourage him to ask you a question in return.

Some questions you could ask

- What do you enjoy most about being a father?
- In what ways does the family bring you joy?
- What can I do to help relieve the stress in your life?
- Why do you believe in Christ?
- What is most important about your faith?
- How do you feel about living in this city and neighborhood?
- What do you hope your life will be like in ten years?

82 **Plan a vacation.**

Visit a travel agent and collect travel brochures from all over the country and the world. Lay them out on a table. Give your husband a sheet of paper and a pen, and have him list his top ten vacation spots. Allow him to add those that aren't represented by brochures. Afterward, see how his list compares to yours. Then talk about how you might be able to visit one or more of the locations on which you agree.

**BONUS
IDEA!**

Listen to what he tells the dog.

83 **Buy a calendar.**

Get an inexpensive calendar or photocopy the next month and give it to your husband. Ask him to fill in all his major events and activities so that you can know what to expect and to help you plan your schedule. When he has finished, talk about when you can take family outings, go out as a couple, go on an escape weekend, etc. (Note: You may have to do this three months in advance to find a free weekend.)

84 **Play the Ungame.**

Christian bookstores and many other stores sell the Ungame. This board game is designed to foster discussion among people. Play it as a family or as a couple.

85 **Eat in the other room.**

Feed the kids first, in the kitchen as usual. Then invite your husband into the dining room and eat with him there—just the two of you. If you don't have a separate dining room, set the table with a tablecloth, flowers, and candles; turn the lights down; and play soft music. That setting will be much more conducive to conversation, especially if you can put your children to bed or send them out to their evening's activities before you and your husband have dinner!

BONUS IDEA!

Spend a weekend hiking together in a state park.

86 Check 'em out.

When you're at the airport, in a shopping mall, or in another situation where you can observe a crowd, look for people who fit certain stereotypes. Talk about why these people appear to fit the stereotypes.

Variation I: If you've recently read a novel together, you could pretend you're from Central Casting and find people to play each character. *Variation II:* Make up a story based on the people you see.

Some characters you might see in a crowded place

- psychiatrist
- foreign agent
- fashion model
- professional football player
- aging hippie
- minister
- librarian
- drug dealer
- novelist
- big-city mayor

87 **Write a letter.**

Write your feelings, thoughts, and questions in a long letter to your husband. Then mail it to him at his office. In the letter you can ask for a reply on the phone, in the mail, or in person. (Don't try this unless you're sure your husband opens his own mail!)

BONUS IDEA!

Give him a back rub.

88 **Give feedback.**

When your husband tells you something, especially when he is
expressing an opinion, don't interrupt him. Listen quietly and
then feed back to him what you hear him saying, even if you
don't agree. For example, if he says something like, "I can't
believe those politicians in Washington—they're all a bunch of
crooks!" you could say something like, "It sounds like you
don't trust politicians." Your attitude will help create a positive
atmosphere for communication. In fact, what begins as
superficial talk on one topic can turn into a deep discussion on
another.

89 **Do a puzzle.**

Buy a 1,000-piece jigsaw puzzle and put it together with your husband. As you're searching for the right pieces, you'll have plenty of opportunities to talk about all sorts of things.

90 Go for a walk.

Many men find it difficult to talk at home, where there are so many distractions. If that's the case with your husband, get him away from the house by going on a walk or bike ride. During the walk, you should be able to find plenty of things to talk about.

BONUS IDEA!

Go with him to his high-school reunion.

91 **Organize the pictures.**

Gather the snapshots you've taken over the past few years, organize them, select the best ones, and put them in an album. Spend some time after dinner some evening going through the album with your husband. This is sure to spark nostalgic conversation. Then talk about important family events coming up in the next weeks and months. What pictures will you be wanting to take to include in your album?

92 **Soak together.**

Spend an hour or so relaxing in a hot tub with your husband.
Don't have a hot tub? Ask to use a friend's. Go to a motel that
has one. Check local sport-and-fitness centers to see if any are
available. Look in the yellow pages—sometimes you can find
hot tubs for rent.

93 **Paint.**

Do you have a room, ceiling, wall, or fence to paint? Don't do it yourself or ask him to do it—paint it together. As you brush together, use the time to talk. (Note: We don't recommend wallpapering or washing windows together!)

BONUS IDEA!

Play pick-up sticks.

94 **Check out the photo album.**

Get out your wedding pictures and look at them together. Then look at your oldest child's baby book. Follow this with other photo albums. You should have a great time reminiscing.

95 **Take a break.**

Early some morning or on the weekend, go out to breakfast together. Or if you've both put in a hard day's work, go out for dessert. It'll be fun, and when you get away from home you can concentrate on talking and listening.

96 **Plan your finances.**

Go to a financial planner or a financial planning seminar.
Then work on the family finances together. As you design your
budget, you'll have much to talk about. Keep it friendly!

Buy and read *Getting Your Kid to Talk*, also by Dave Veerman.

97 **Do a project.**

Choose a hobby or a project around the house that you can enjoy doing together. As you work, you will find plenty of time to talk. And your house will soon look better, too!

Some projects and hobbies

- redecorate a room
- build a stereo system
- refinish furniture
- paint walls
- plant a garden
- weed a garden
- freeze berries
- make a quilt
- wax floors
- frame pictures

98 **Go camping.**

Persuade your husband to take off a weekend or more and take the family camping. Nothing can stimulate conversation better than sitting around the fire on a cool, clear night with a hot cup of coffee or cocoa.

99 Teach together.

Talk to the Sunday-school superintendent in your church and volunteer for you and your husband to teach a class together. Choose any age level where there's a need and where you have an interest, from preschoolers to adults. You and your husband will be together both while you teach and while you prepare for the class. And you will undoubtedly spend time talking about the class and its members.

100 Share his interest.

Work at understanding your husband's hobby, sport, and other interests. For example, if he loves football
- learn the rules of the game
- read up on the major players
- keep up with who's winning and losing
- watch games with him

101 **Go high tech.**

The pony express is history. Use today's methods to communicate with your husband.

- Leave a message on his office voice mail.
- Send him a fax (keeping in mind that other people may also read it!).
- Write him a letter on your home or office computer, and send him the file by modem.
- If he's out of town, send him a note and a snack by overnight delivery.
- Leave him a message on your home computer that will show up when he turns the computer on.

Additional titles from Dave Veerman

GETTING YOUR KID TO TALK
(New! Spring 1994)   0-8423-1326-5
100+ ideas to get conversations
going with your kids.

FROM DAD WITH LOVE
(New! Spring 1994)
With Chuck Aycock   0-8423-1333-8
Raise confident kids by giving them
priceless, character-building gifts.

HOW TO APPLY THE BIBLE
0-8423-1384-2
Proven techniques for applying
God's Word—based on the *Life
Application Bible.*

**THE ONE YEAR BIBLE
MEMORY BOOK FOR
FAMILIES**   0-8423-1387-7
Daily verses, review questions, and
notes help families memorize and
understand Scripture.